INTRODUCTION

My name is Mark Rush and I've been drawing and painting since my youth. The illustrations in this coloring book are a collection of sketches I have done over the years. When I get a chance to sketch landscapes, architecture, or just an interesting scene from my travels, I draw in pencil then later fill it in with pen and ink. Many of my compositions I'll do paintings from. I've found that using colored pencils to record the colors is very satisfying and consequently I came up with this book which is a compilation of sketches done over the years. There are many different adult coloring books on the market for flowers, geometric designs, etcetera, but this book offers a unique set of drawings that hopefully stimulates your mind and puts you in another place for a period of time.

Hopefully you enjoy my compositions and find time to create your own color schemes to complete them or use the reference color sketches as a guide line. Colored pencils are lighter then paint and can be used in layers to increase intensity and hue. Water color pens or markers can also be used, but are less forgiving if you make a mistake. When coloring a sky you can use a light blue for a solid cloudless sky, or you can leave areas of white indicating clouds. Yellow, orange and red can be used for sunsets or sunrises. Water can have shades of greens and blues and often reflect the color of the sky. So use your imagination. It's up to you. Vegetation can include yellows, greens, blues, browns and various flowers of multiple colors. Shading can provide dramatic effects keeping in mind where the sun or light source is. Rock layers and geological formations provide a multitude of colors and contrast.

If you're an aspiring artist, hopefully these drawings give you an idea on what a good composition consists of and then you can follow up by sketching your own and use the same coloring techniques applied here to complete them. I find artwork to be very satisfying, and at the end of a stressful day the answer to achieving some peace of mind.

If interested in my work you can contact me at markrushart@gmail.com, or to view my online gallery at http://mark-rush.artistwebsites.com.

INDEX OF ILLUSTRATIONS V2

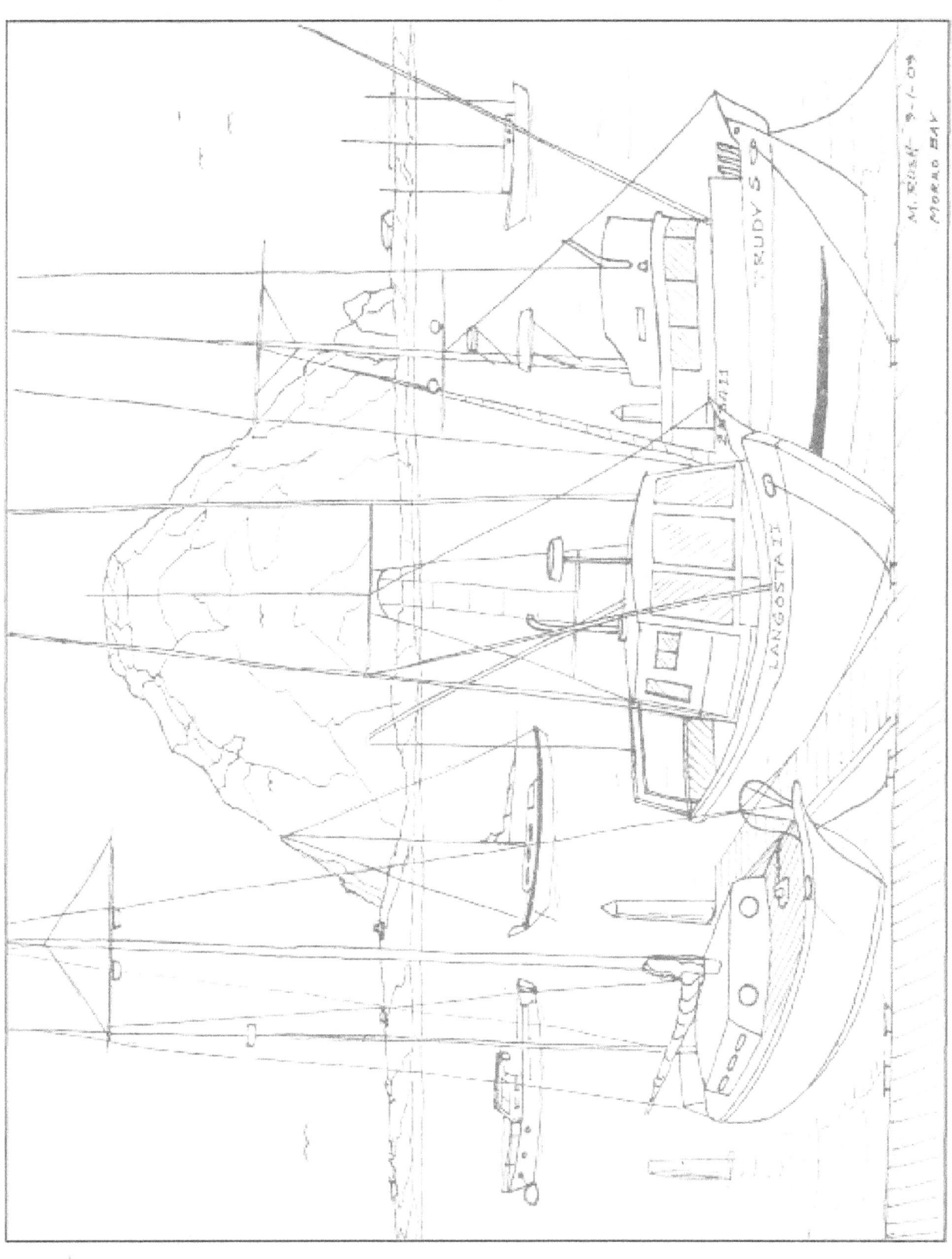

M. RUSK 9-1-04
MORRO BAY

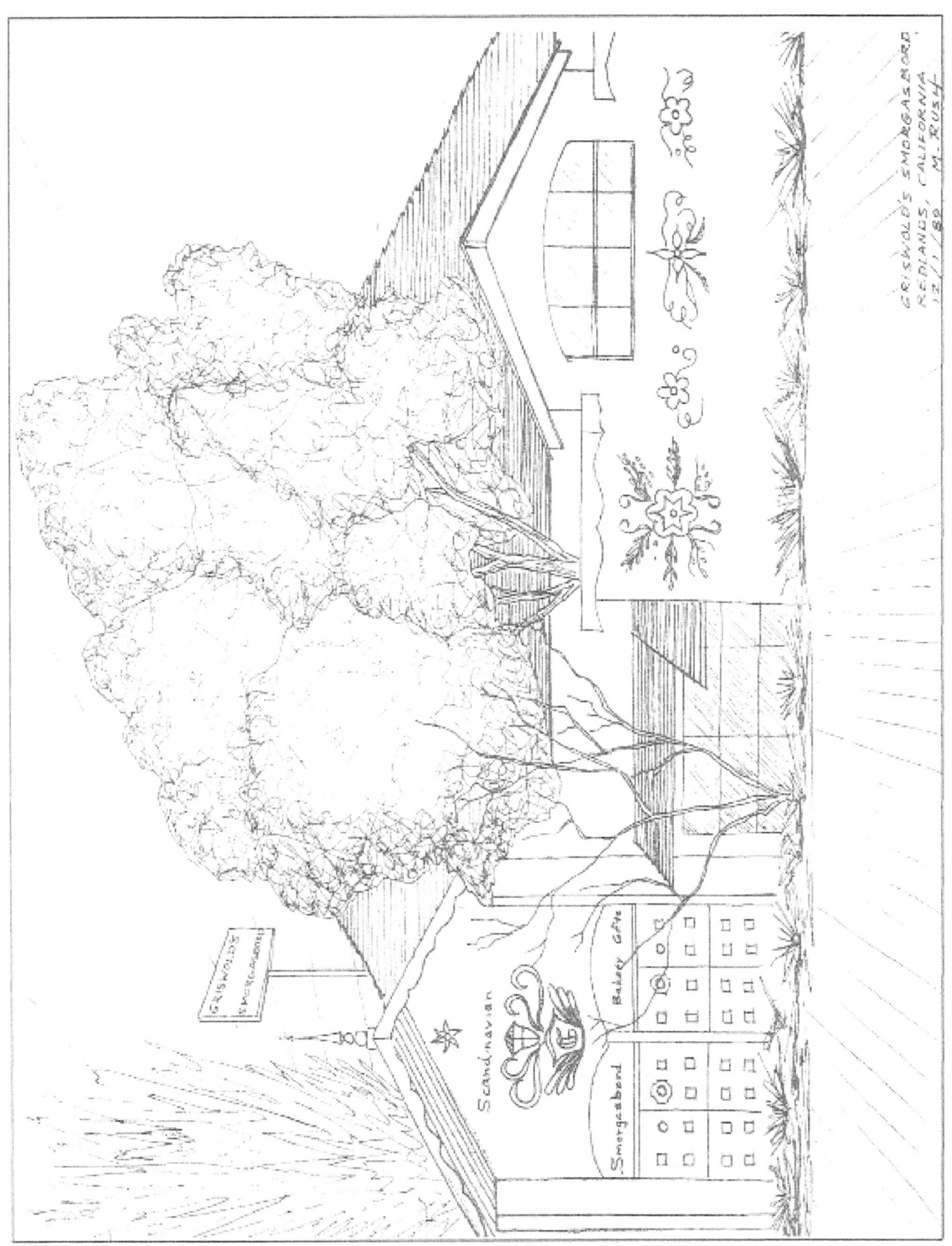

GRISWOLD'S SMORGASBORD
REDLANDS, CALIFORNIA
12/1/88   M. RUSH

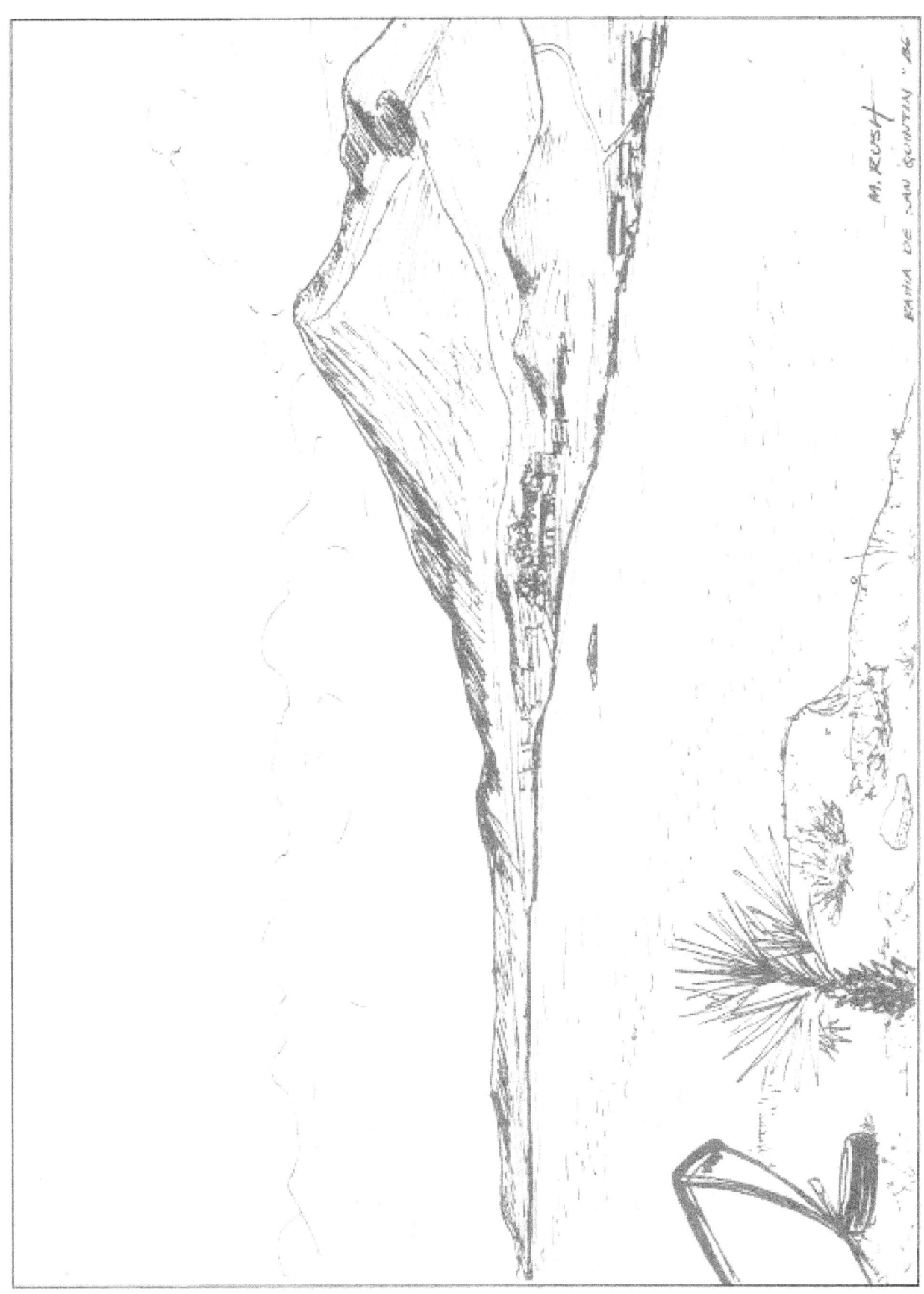

M. RUSH

BAHIA DE SAN QUINTIN '86

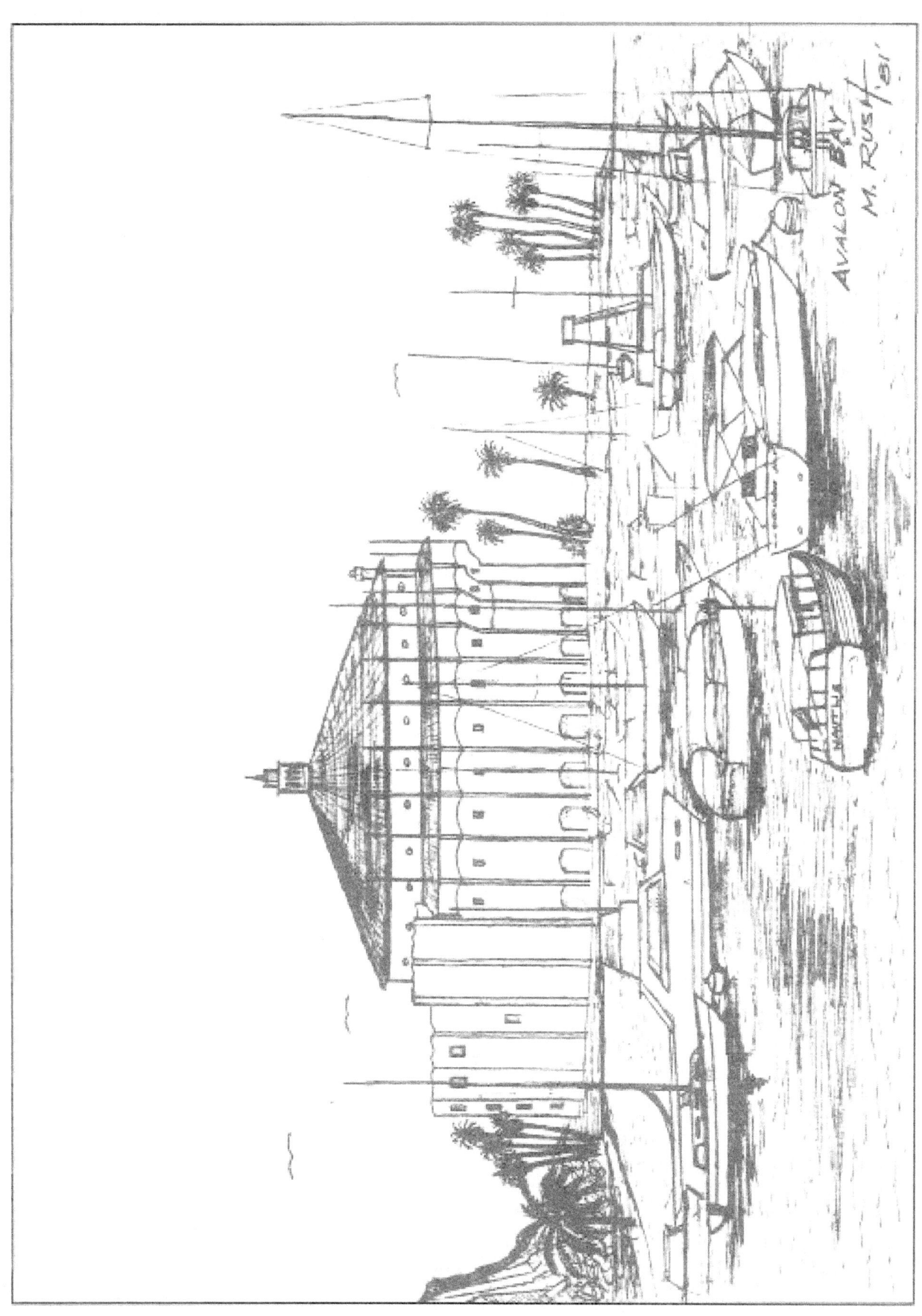

AVALON BAY

M. RUSH / 81

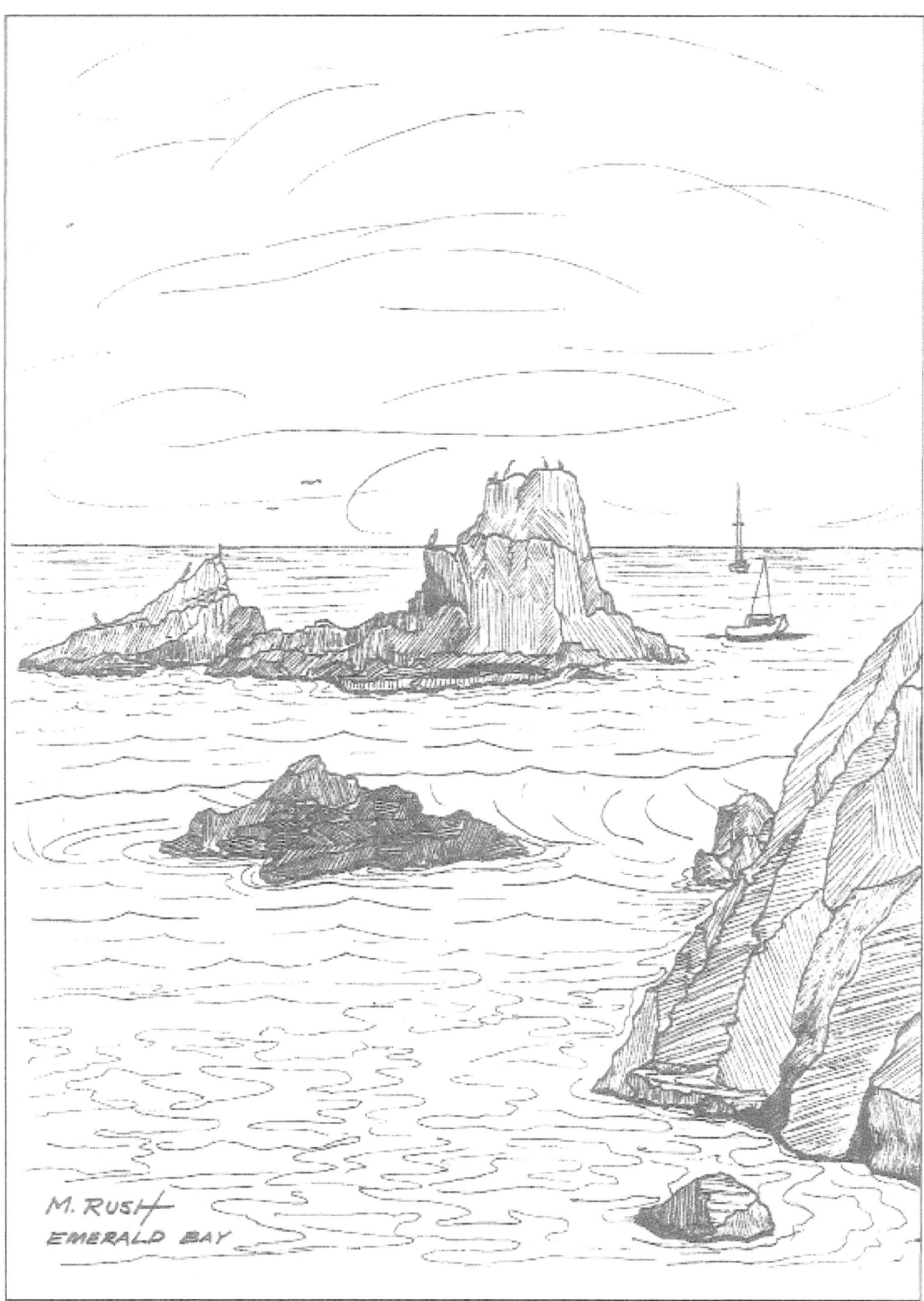

M. RUSH
EMERALD BAY

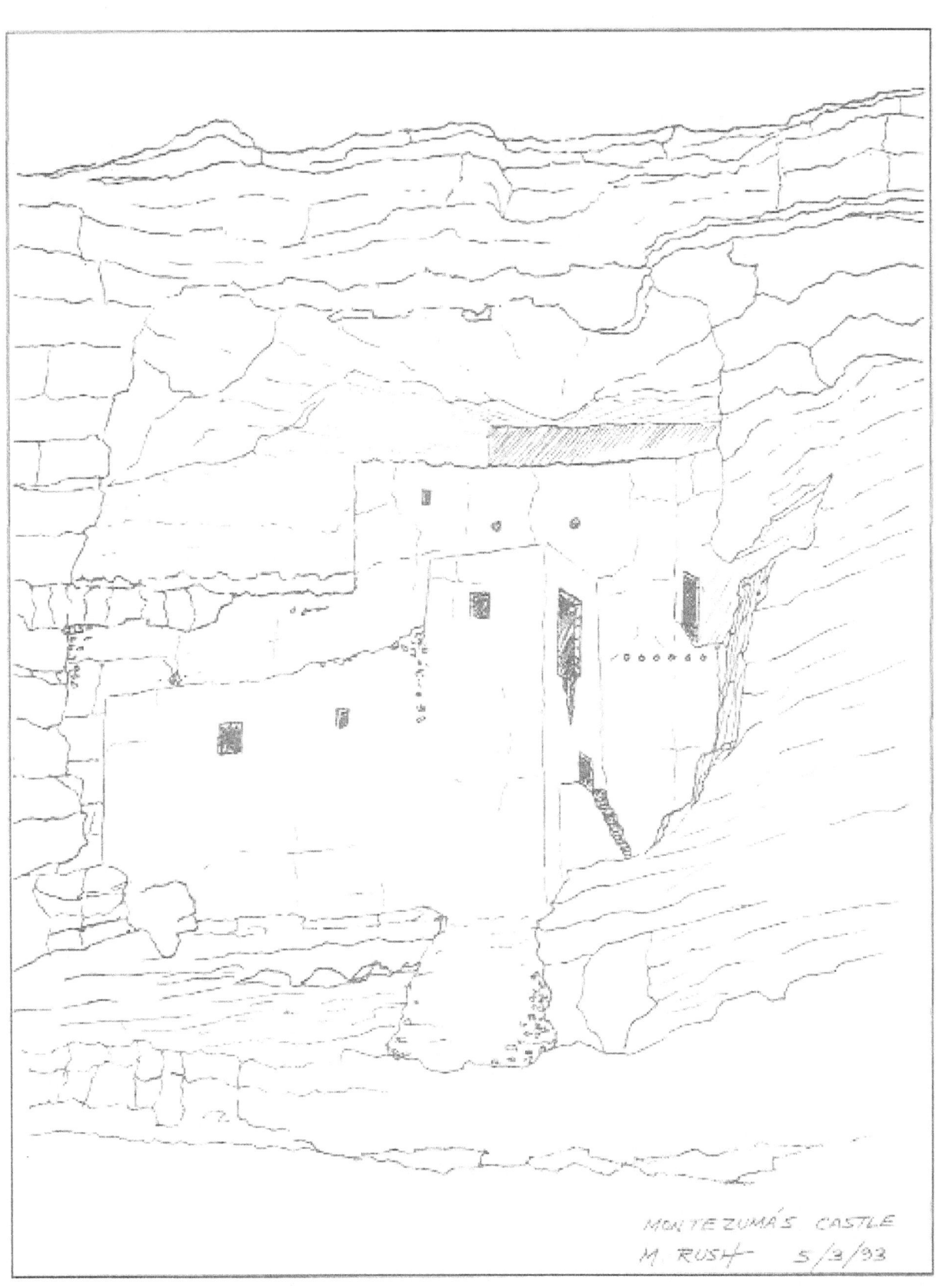

MONTEZUMA'S CASTLE
M RUSH   5/3/93

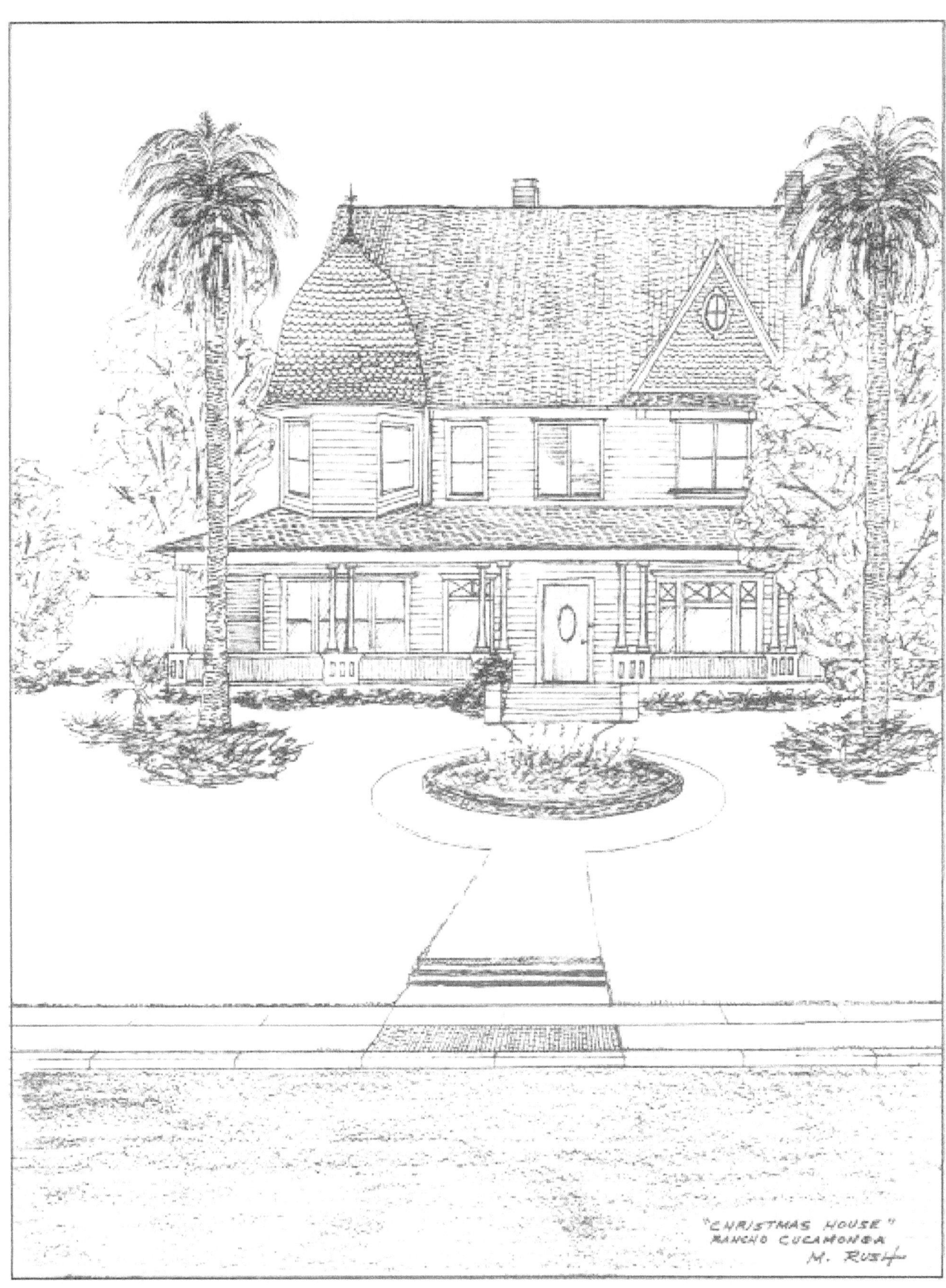

"CHRISTMAS HOUSE"
RANCHO CUCAMONGA
M. RUSH

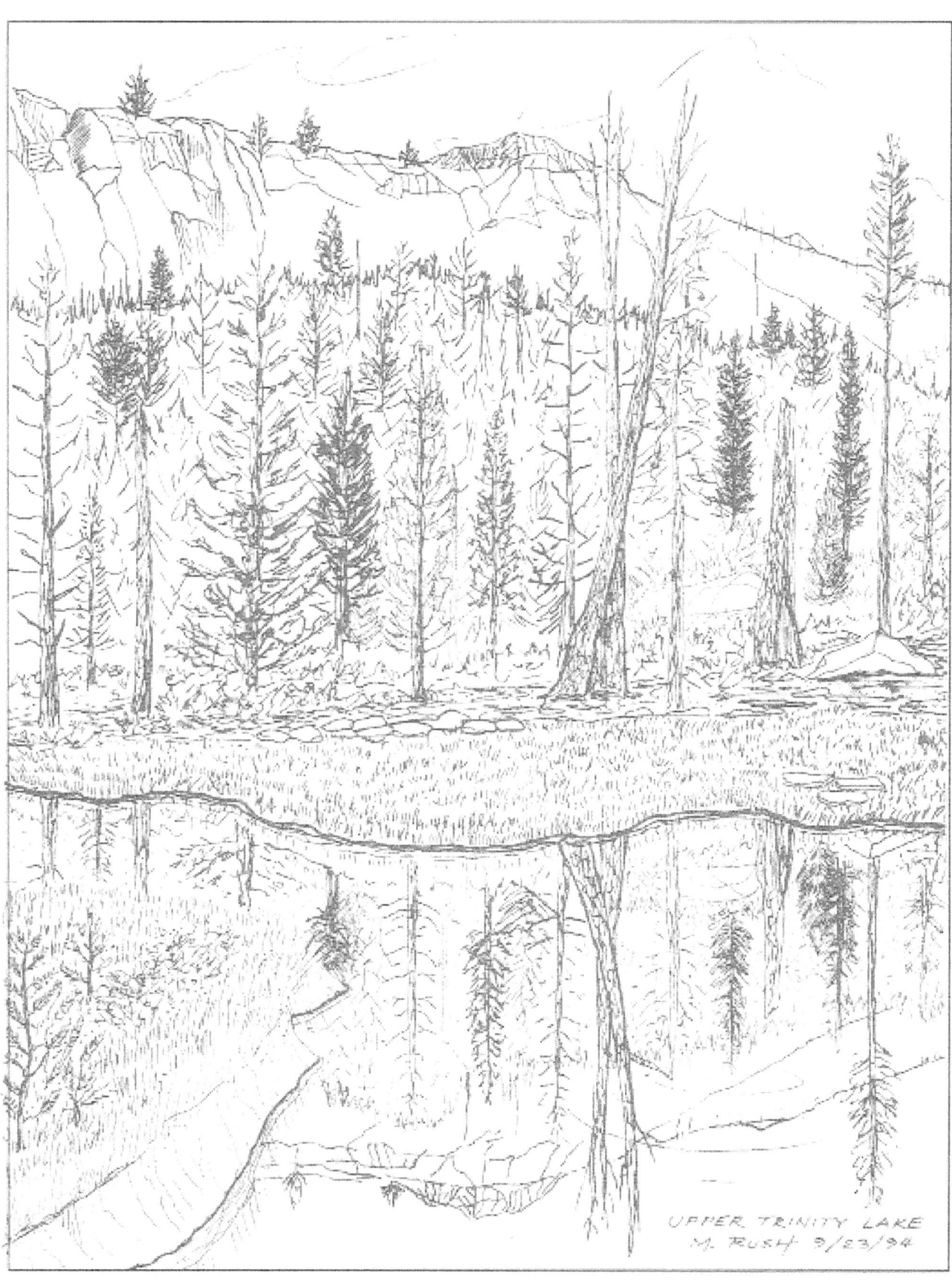

UPPER TRINITY LAKE
M. RUSH 9/23/94

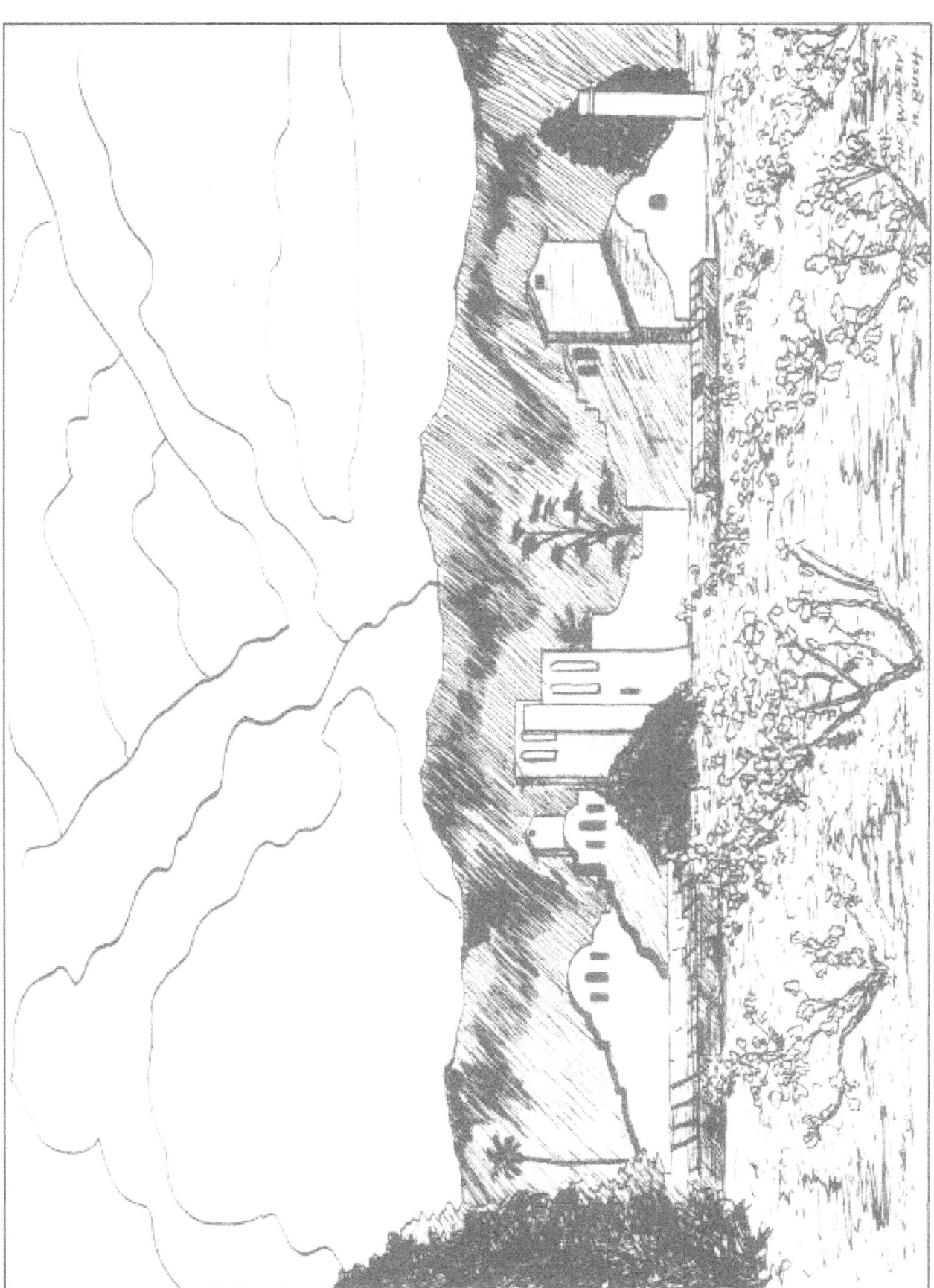

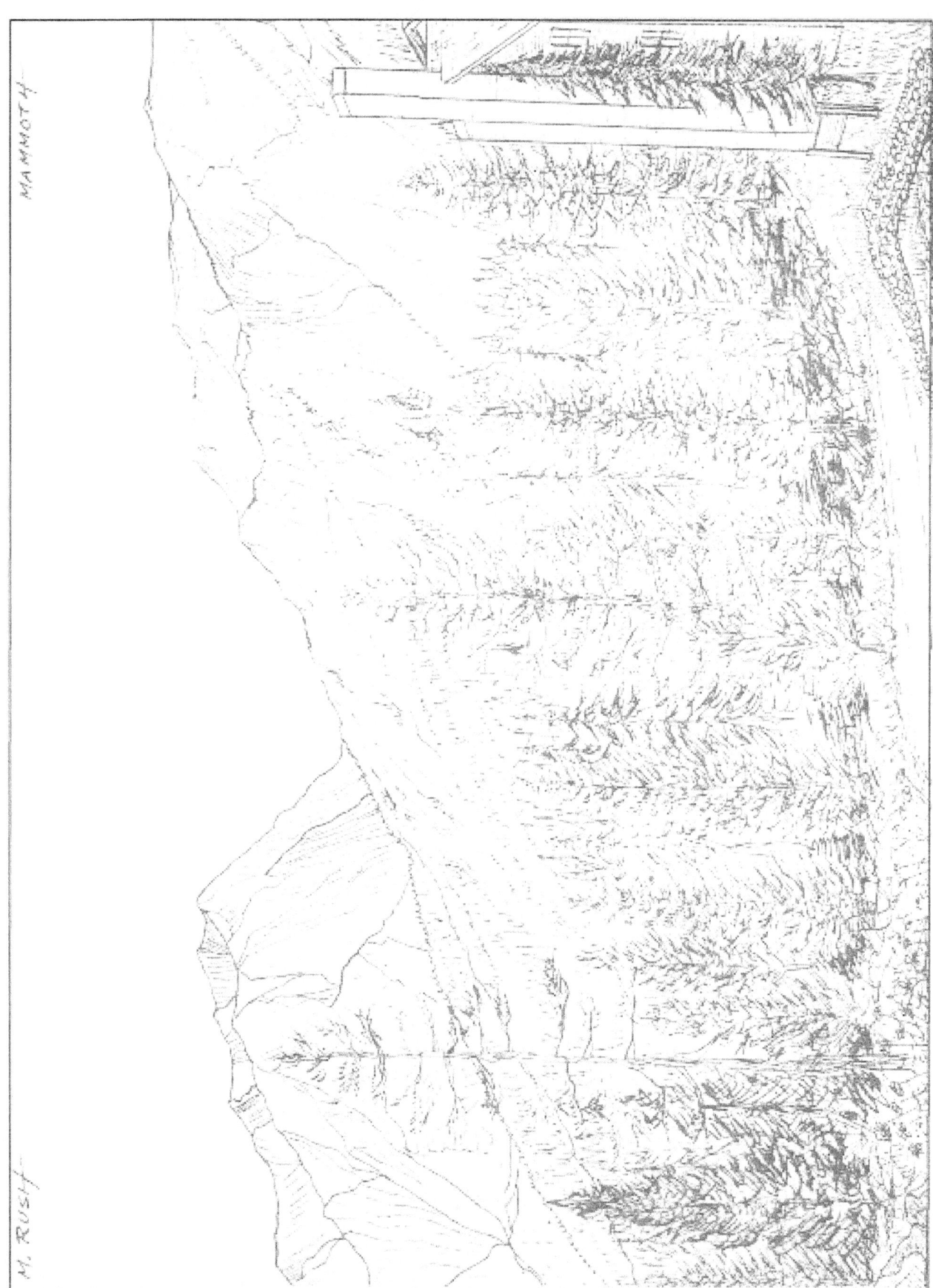

MAMMOTH

M. RUSH

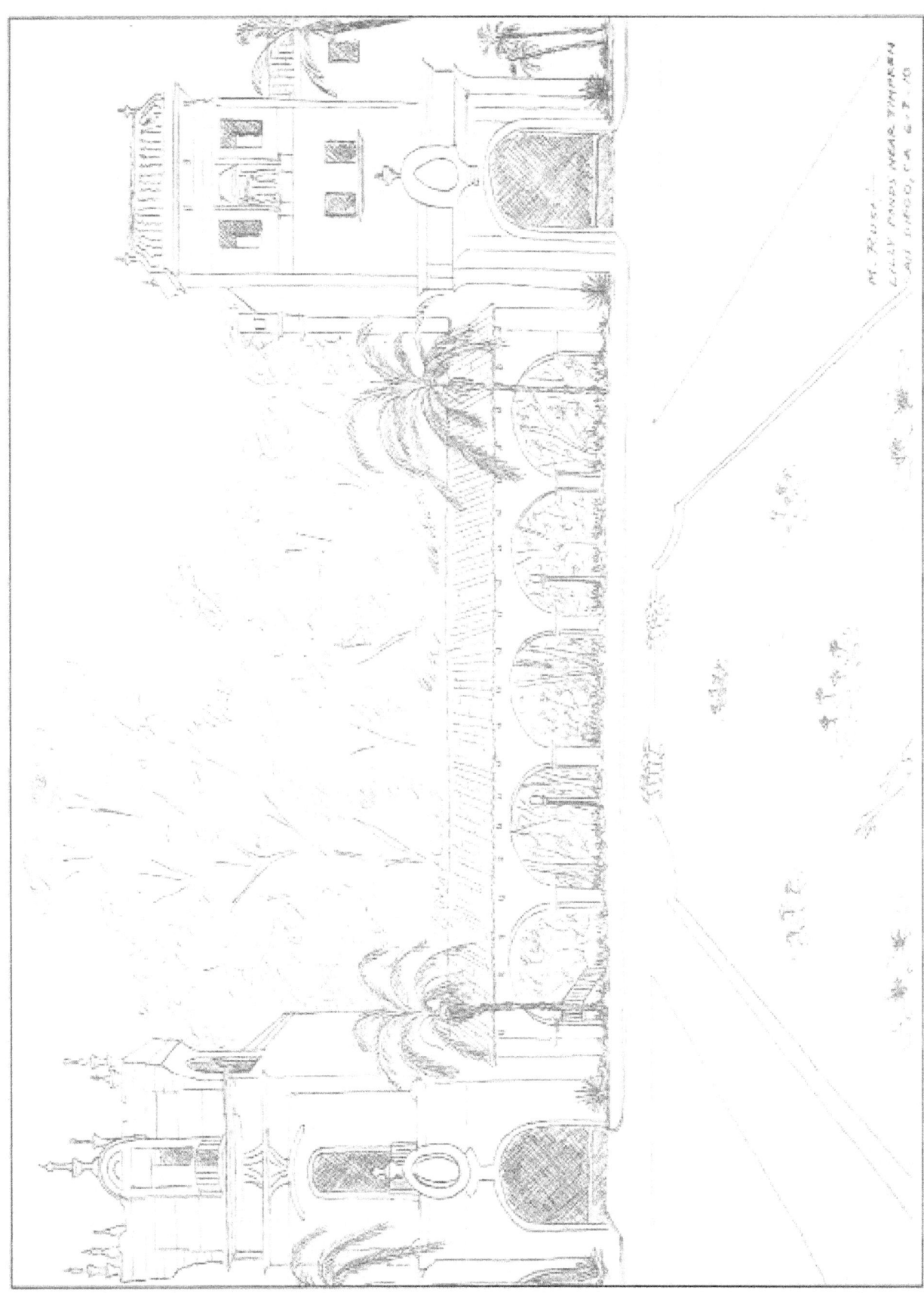

M. RUGA
LILLY PONDS, NEAR TIJUANA
SAN DIEGO, CA 6-7-10

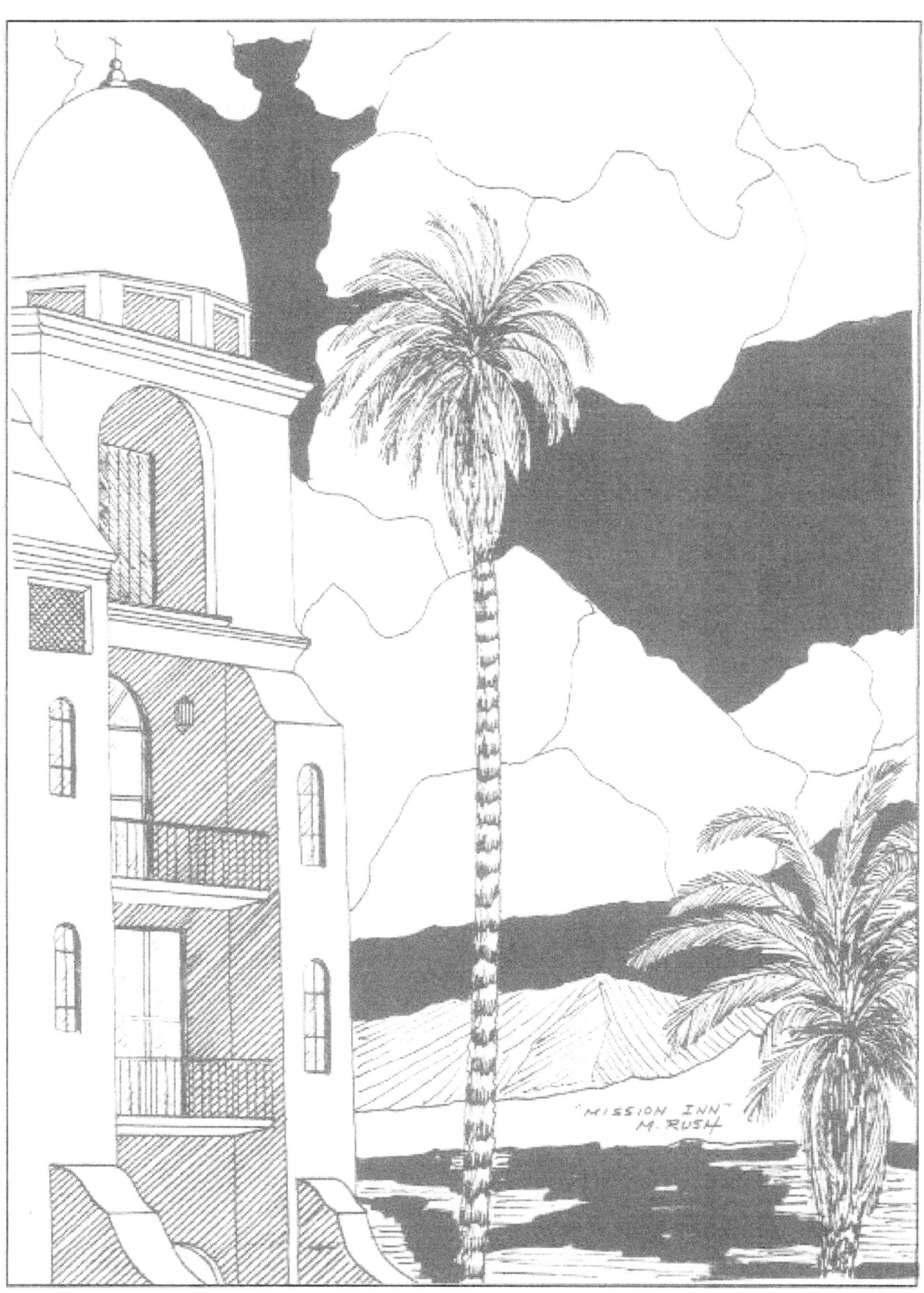

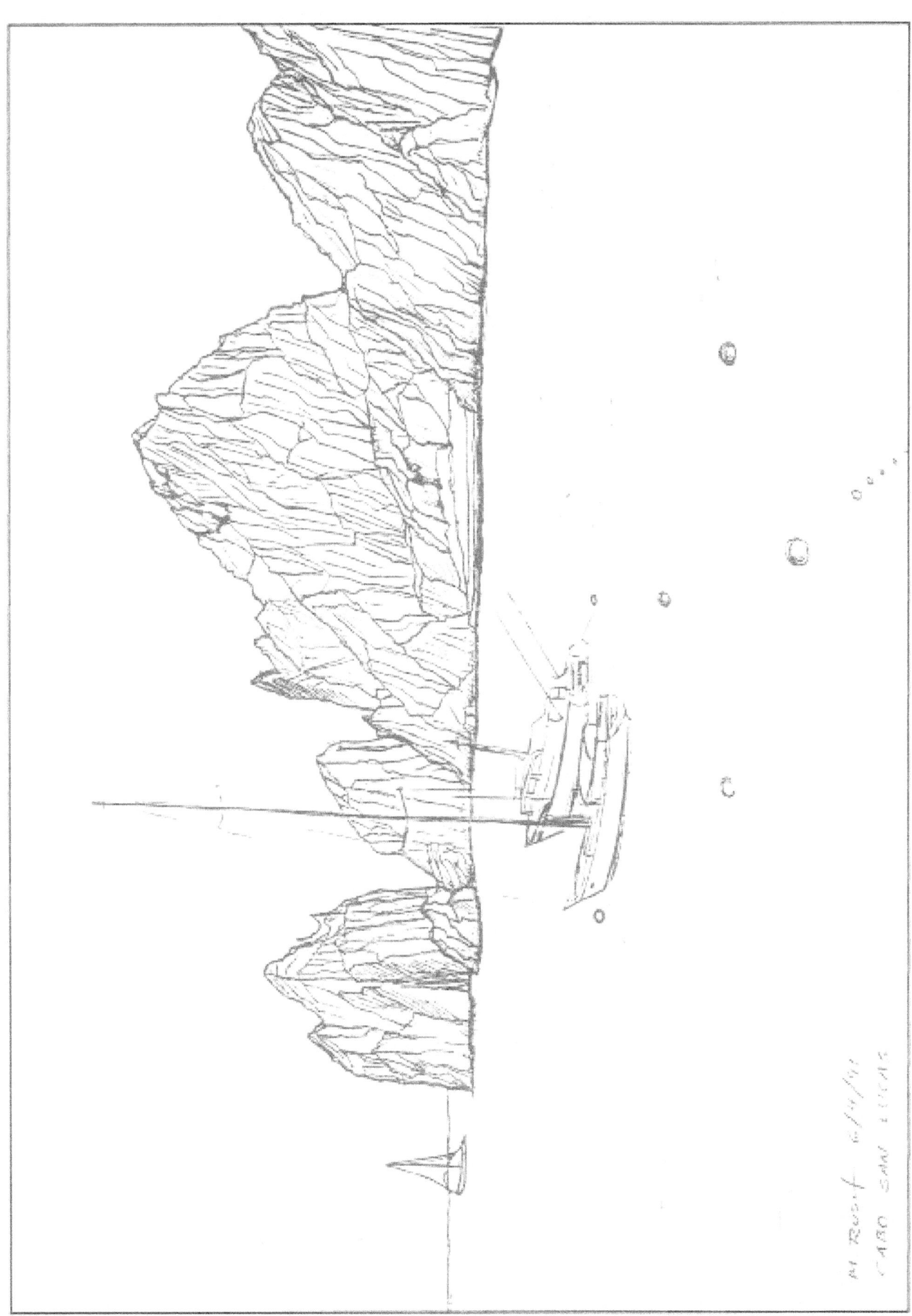

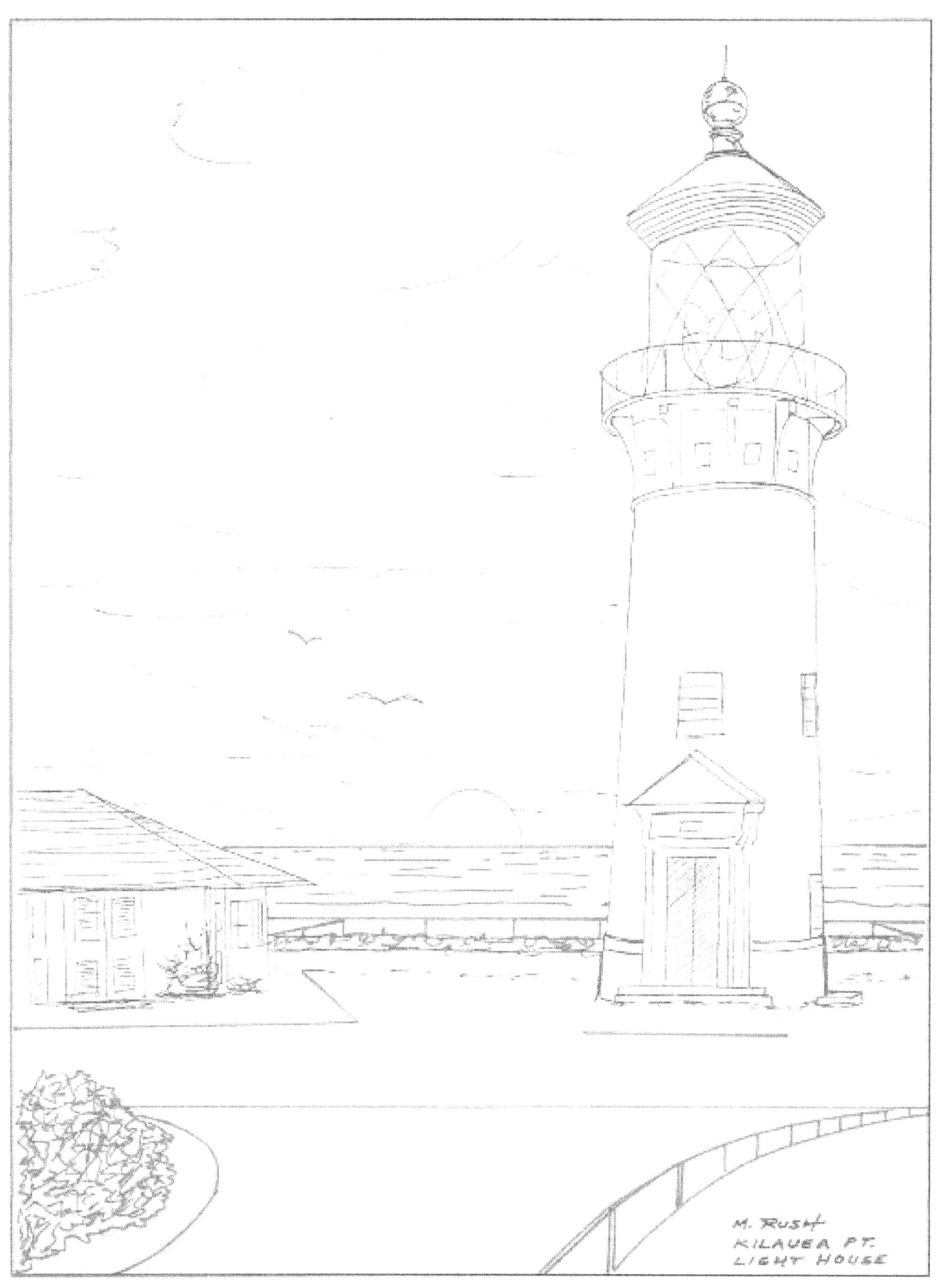

M. RUSH
KILAUEA PT.
LIGHT HOUSE

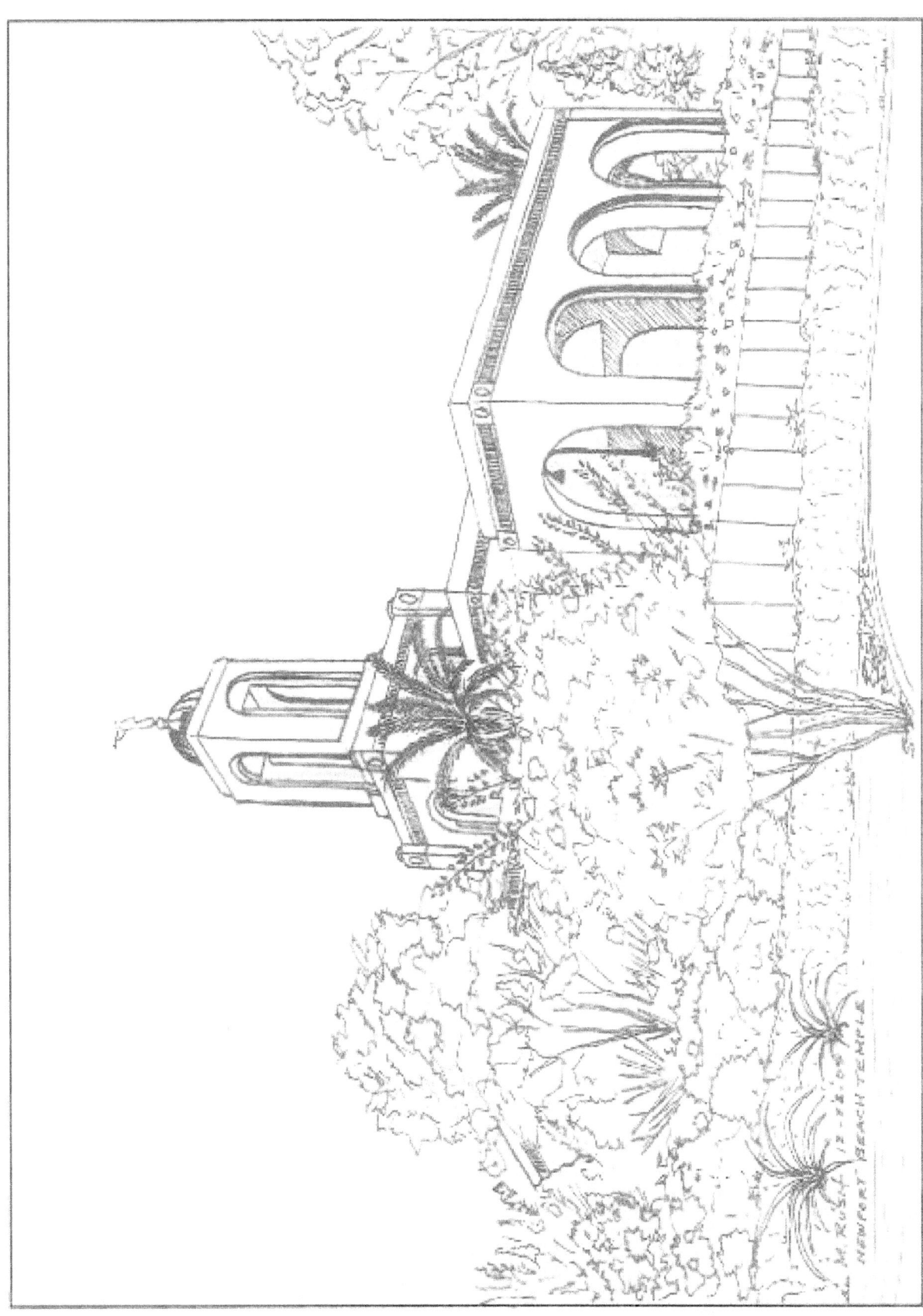

M. ROSEN '12 FROM NEWPORT BEACH TEMPLE

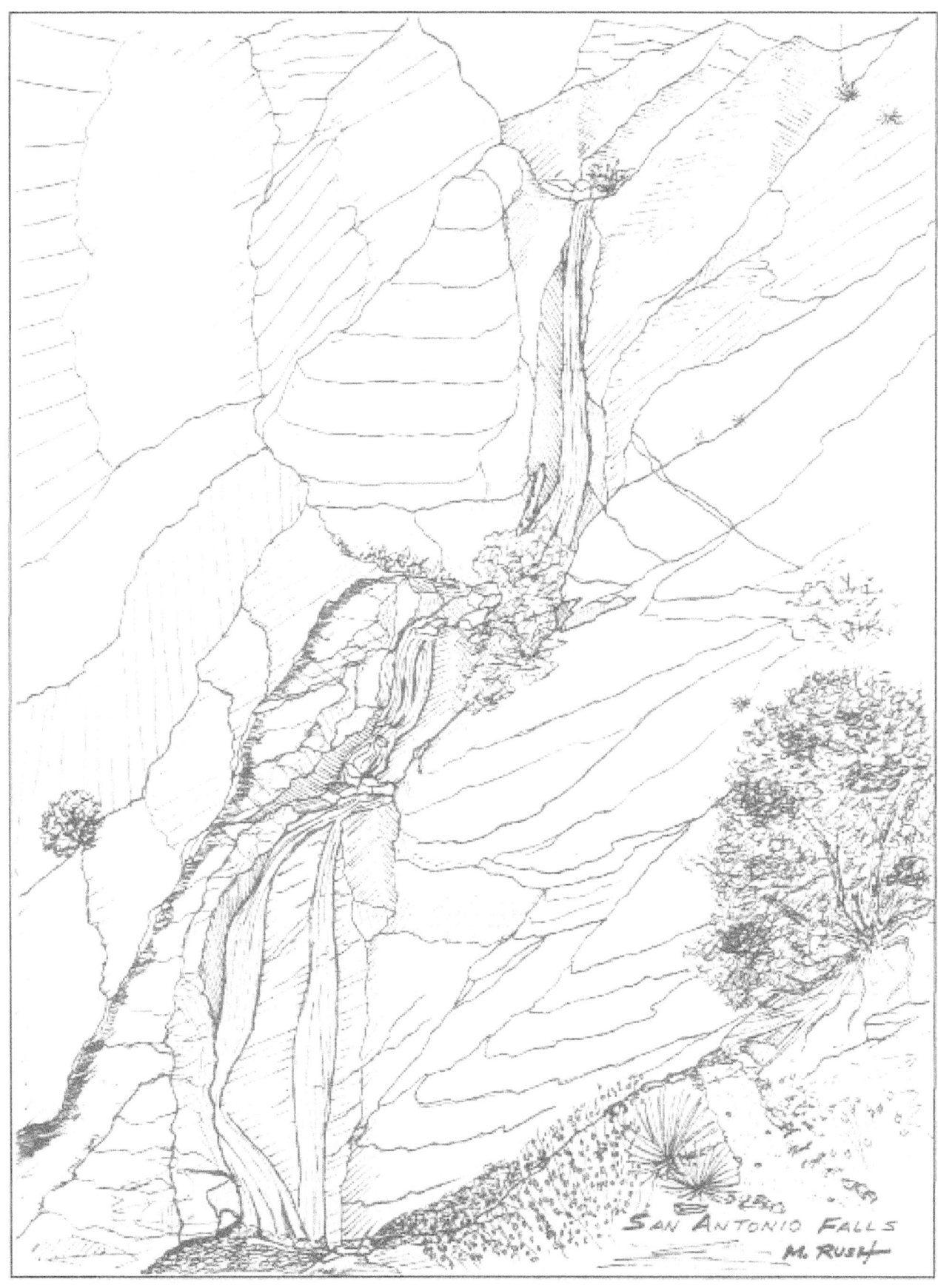

San Antonio Falls

M. Rush

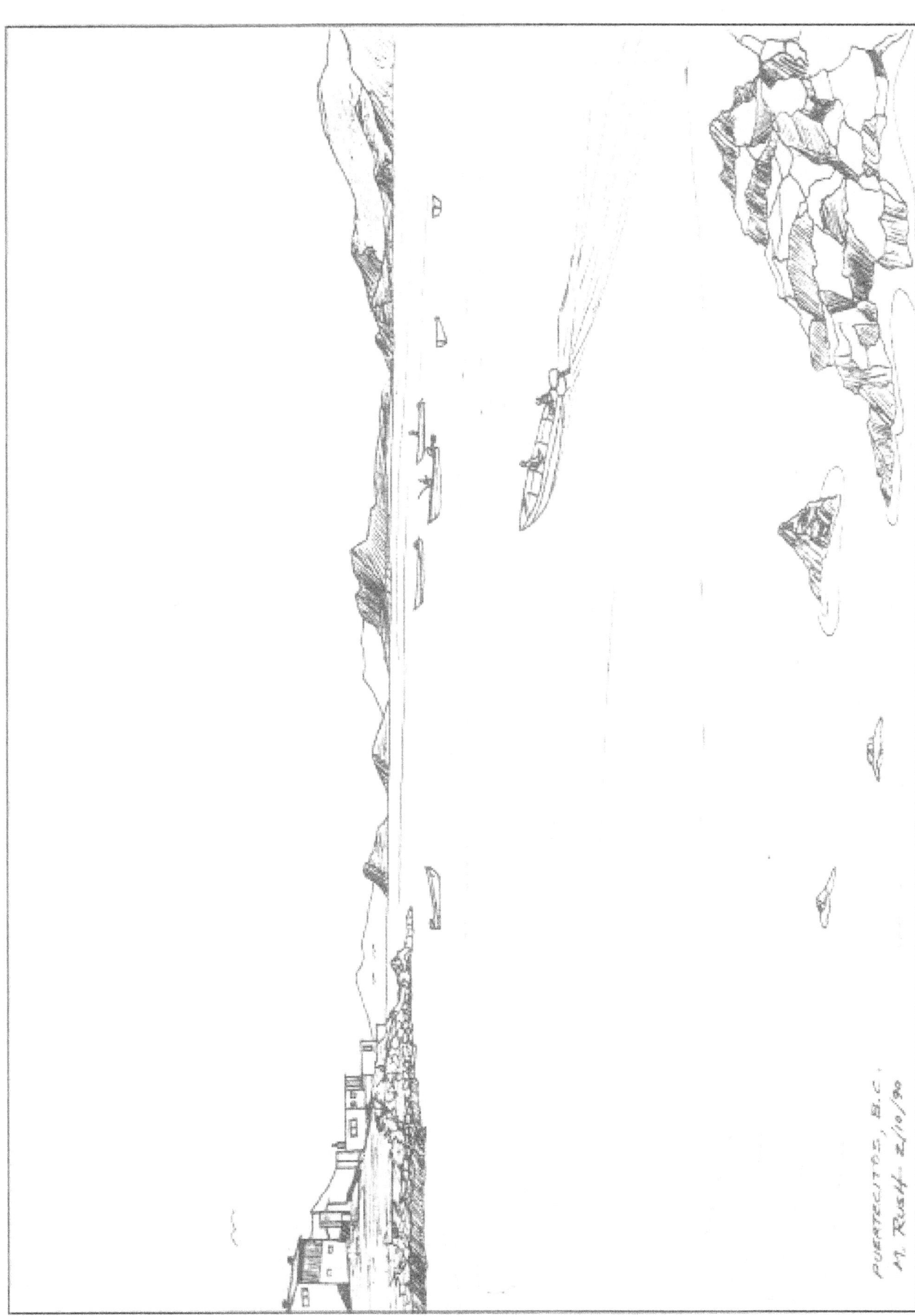

PUERTECITOS, B.C.
M. Rush 2/10/90

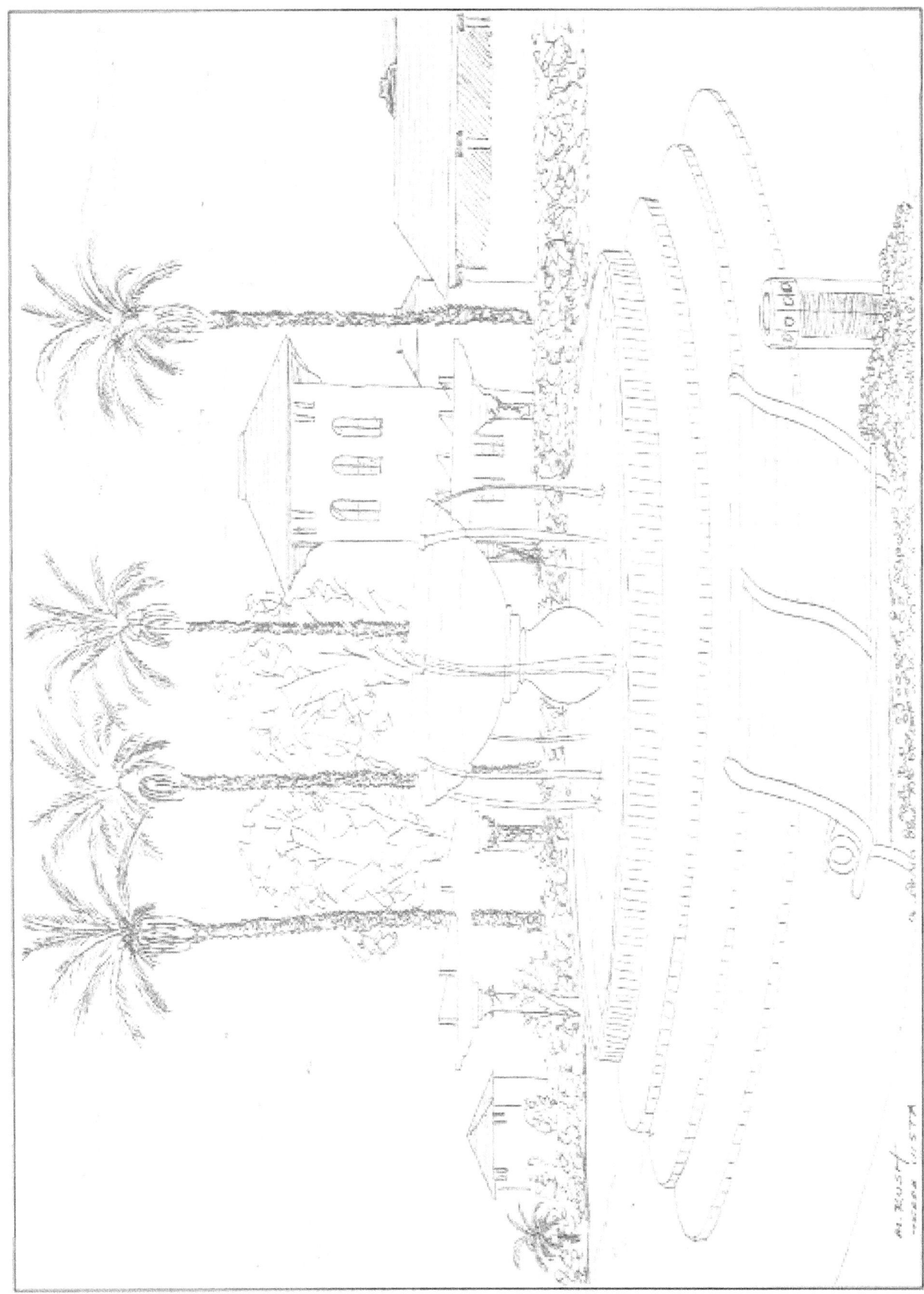

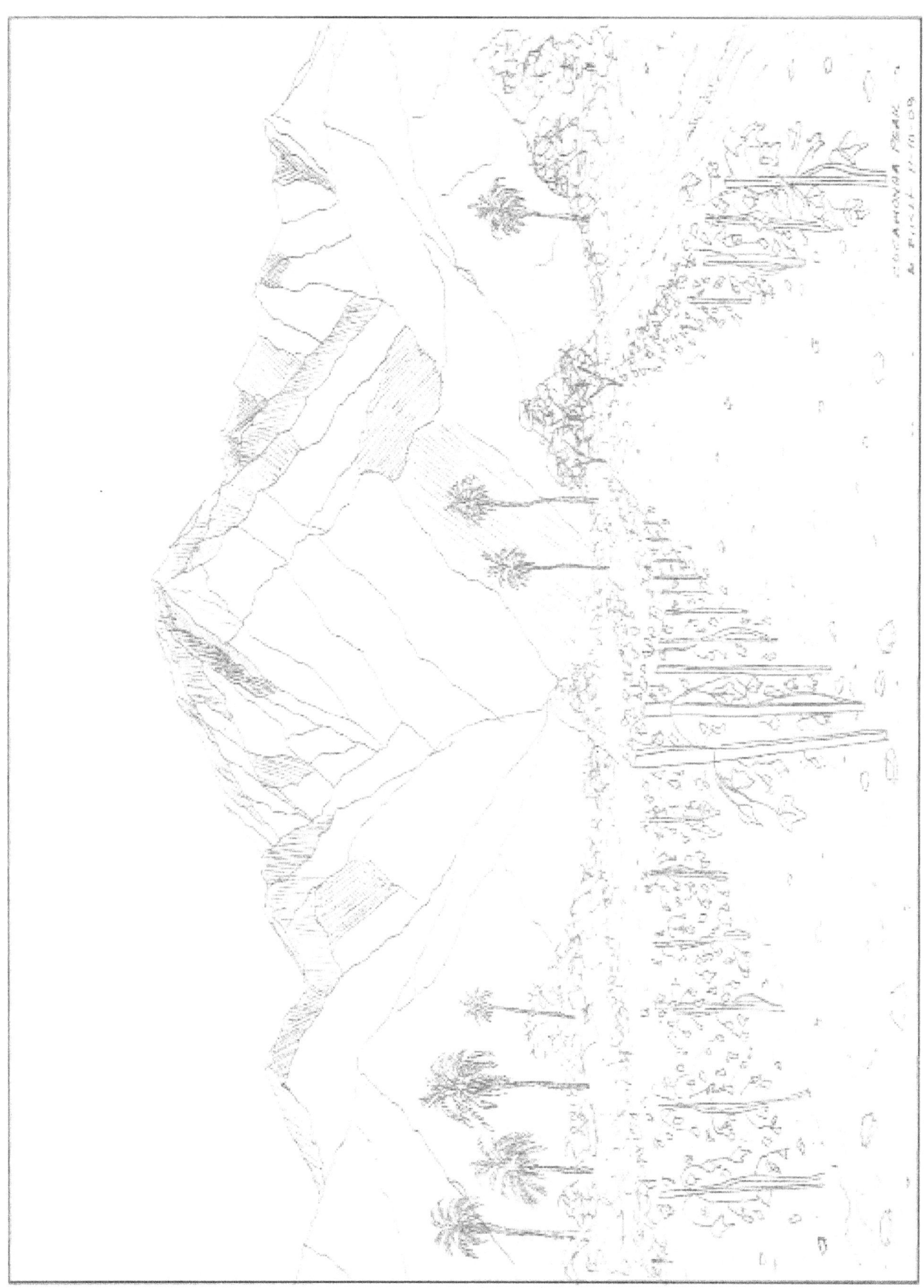

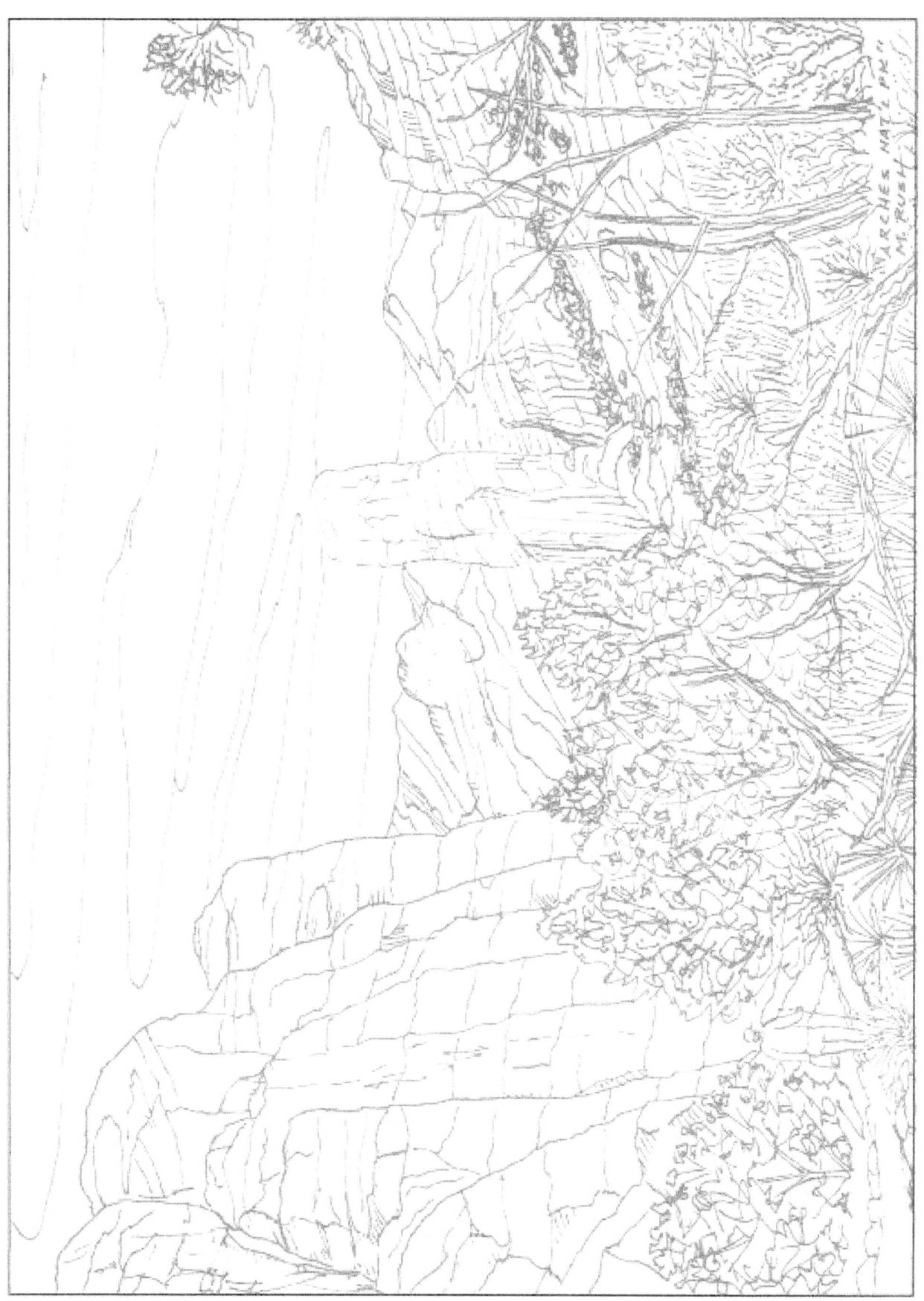

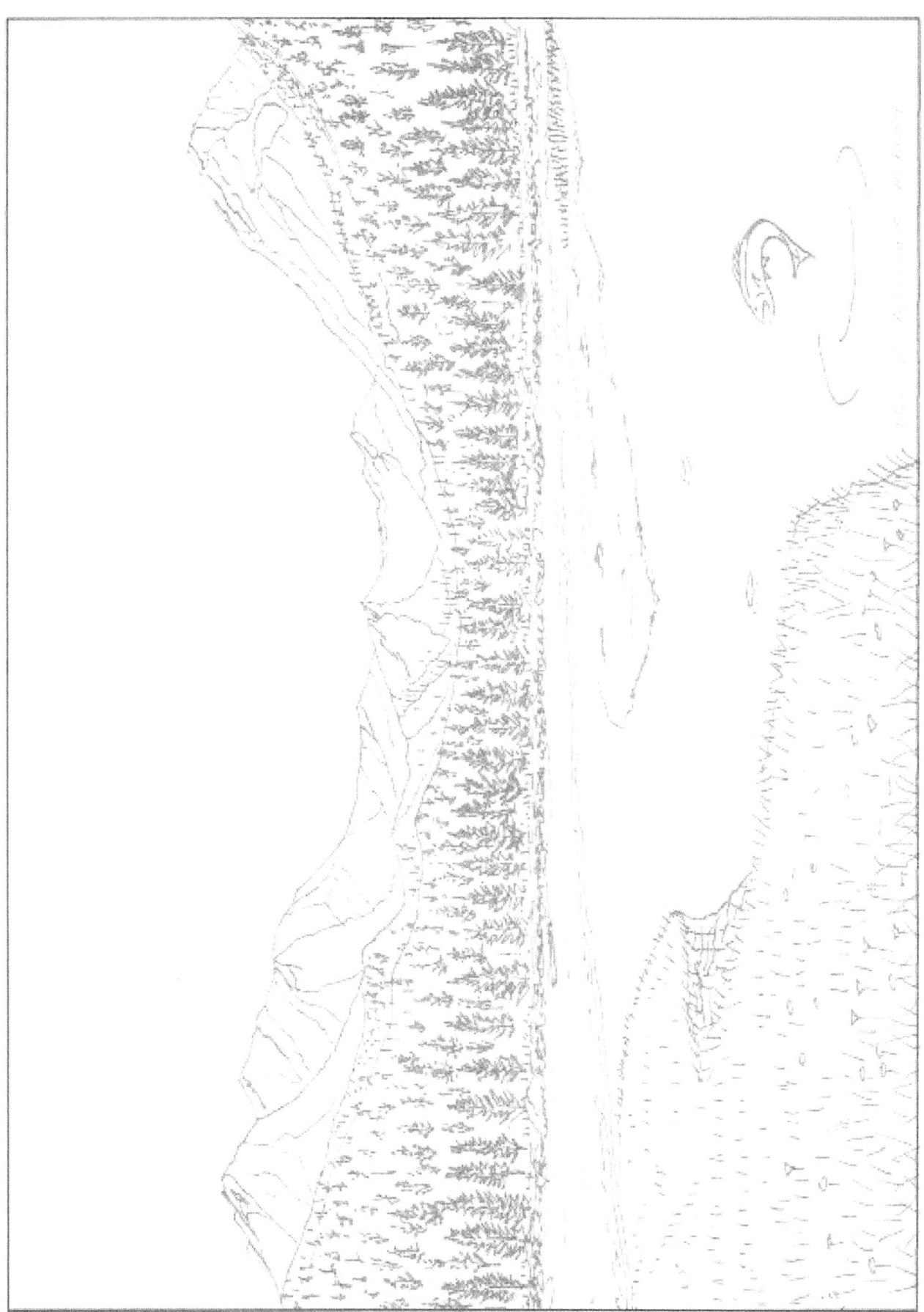

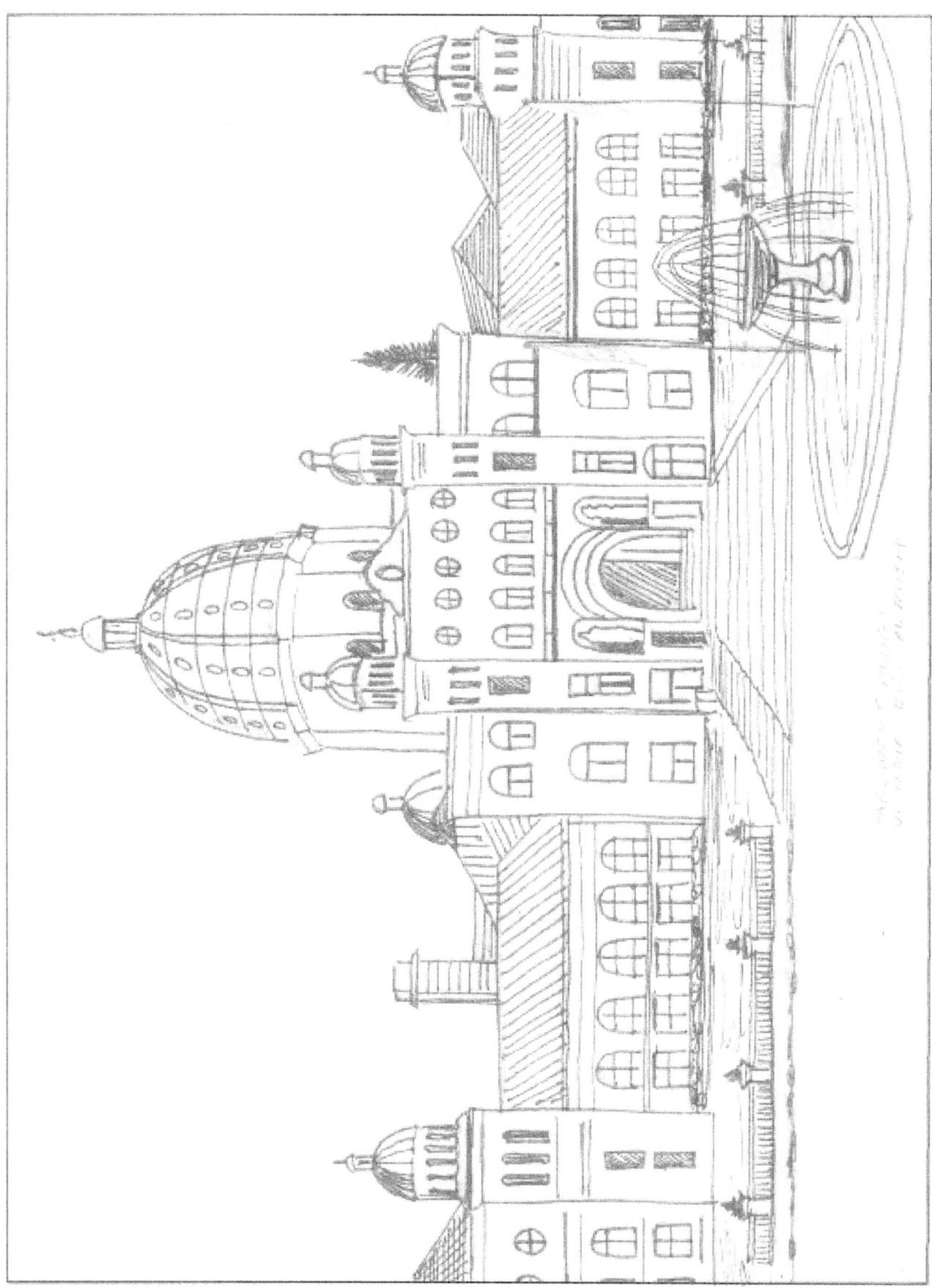

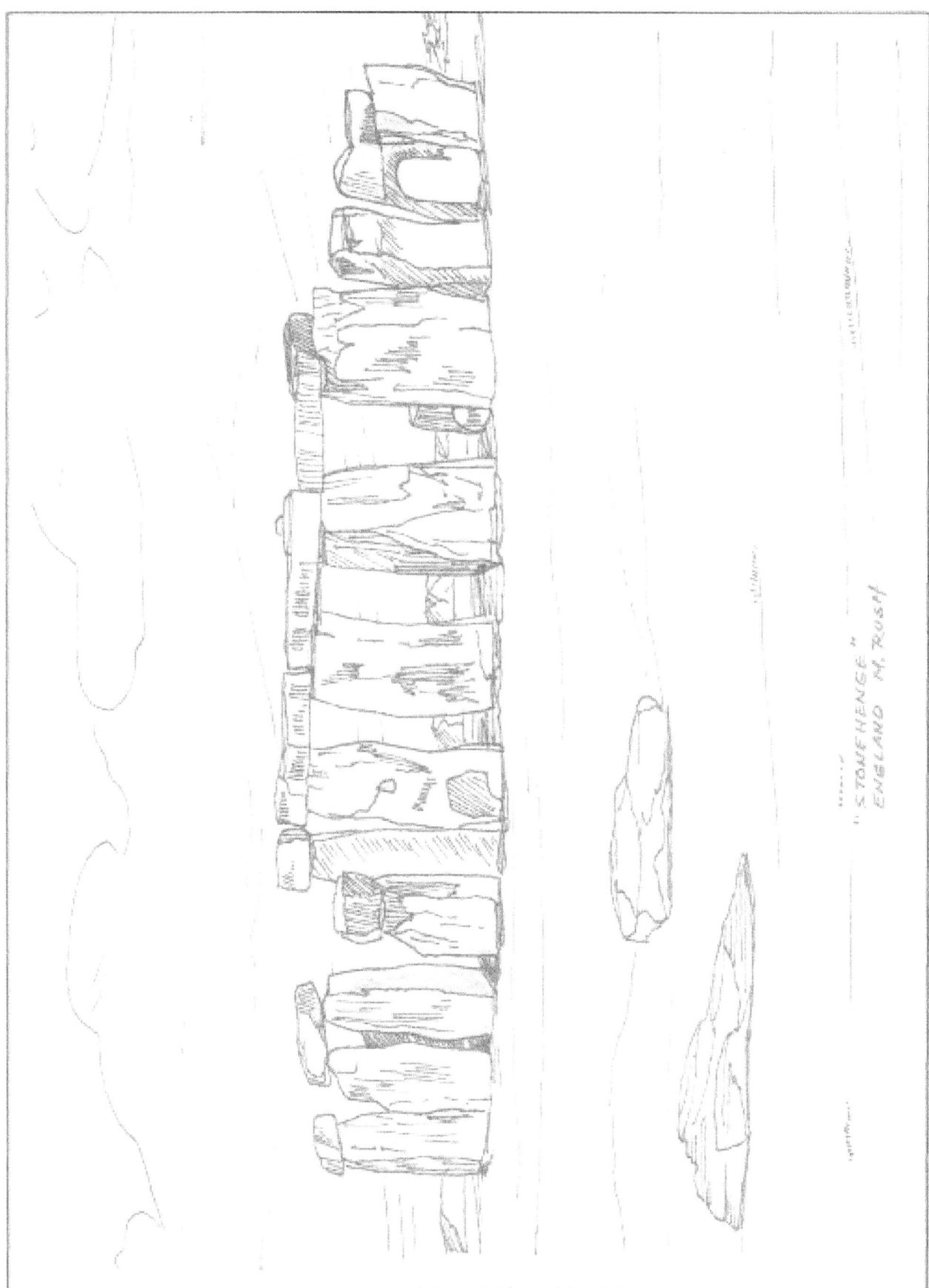

"STONEHENGE"
ENGLAND M. RUSH

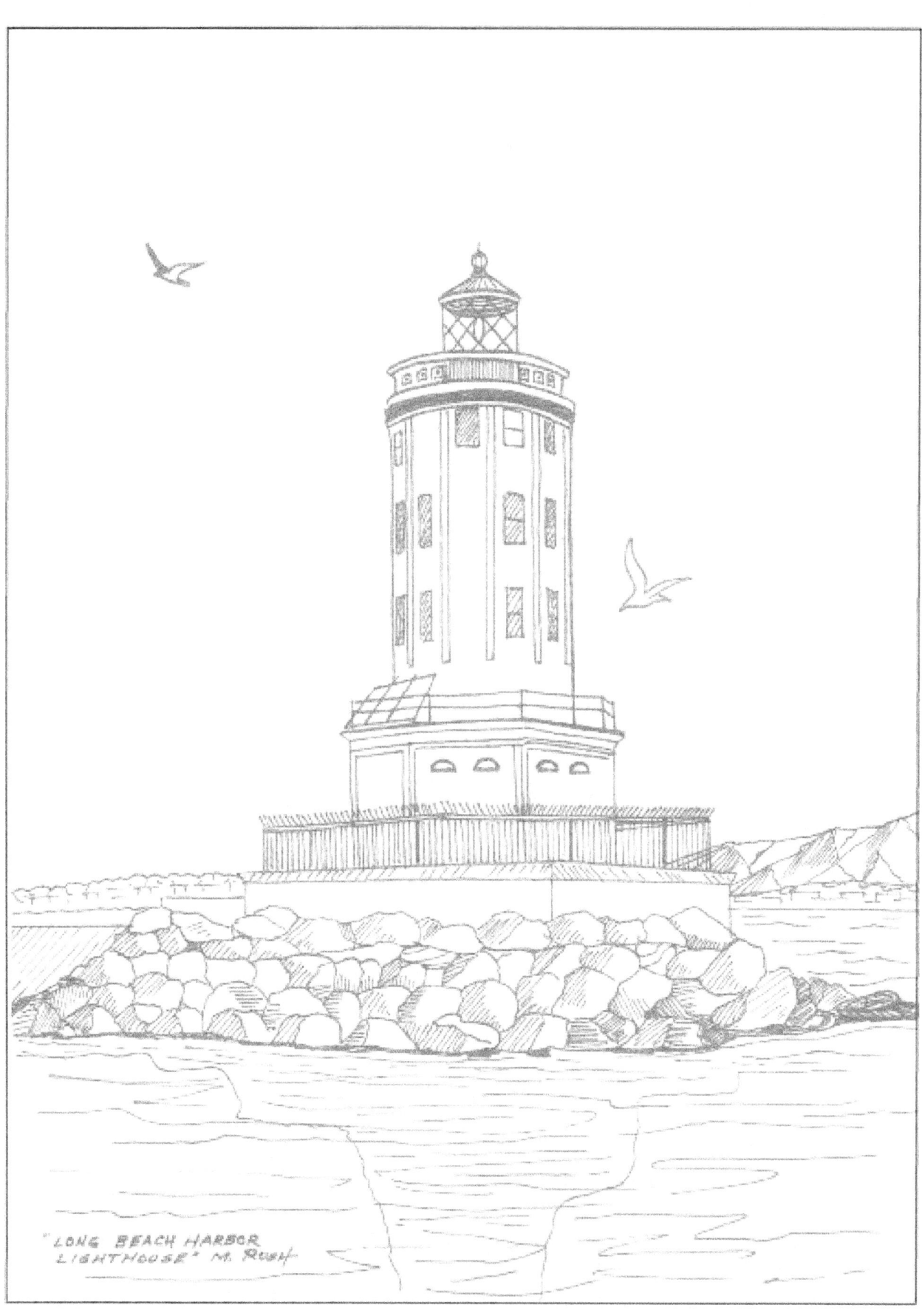

"LONG BEACH HARBOR
LIGHTHOUSE" M. RUSH